PHONICS FOR READING
LEVEL 3

Children's Reading & Writing Education Books

PROFESSOR GUSTO
EDUCATIONAL & INFORMATIVE BOOKS FOR CHILDREN
(PRE-K / K-12)

Read and rewrite the following words.

'c' with a 's' sound

ace   _____

ice   _____

icy   _____

acid   _____

cell   _____

cent   _____

city   _____

'c' with a 's' sound

cyan   _____

dice   _____

face   _____

lace   _____

lice   _____

mice   _____

nice   _____

'ch' with a 'c' sound

ache _____

echo _____

loch _____

chaos _____

chasm _____

choir _____

chord _____

'ch' with a 'c' sound

ochre _____

aching _____

anchor _____

chorus _____

orchid _____

scheme _____

school _____

'ch' with a 'sh' sound

chef

niche

chalet

cloche

quiche

sachet

chassis

'ch' with a 'sh' sound

chateau _____

chicane _____

chiffon _____

crochet _____

machine _____

brochure _____

charades _____

'e_e'

eve

gene

grebe

scene

theme

these

accede

'e_e'

delete _____

impede _____

recede _____

scheme _____

serene _____

athlete _____

compete _____

'g' with a 'j' sound

age

gel

gem

gym

ages

cage

edge

'g' with a 'j' sound

edgy   _____

gent   _____

germ   _____

gist   _____

huge   _____

page   _____

rage   _____

'igh' and 'ight'

high   _____

nigh   _____

sigh   _____

fight   _____

light   _____

might   _____

night   _____

'igh' and 'ight'

right   _____

sight   _____

thigh   _____

tight   _____

alight   _____

blight   _____

bright   _____

'aw'

dawn _____

draw _____

fawn _____

flaw _____

gnaw _____

hawk _____

lawn _____

'aw'

pawn _____

thaw _____

yawn _____

awful _____

brawl _____

crawl _____

drawn _____

'i_e'

ice _____

bide _____

bike _____

bite _____

dice _____

dive _____

file _____

'i_e'

fine _____

five _____

hide _____

hike _____

hive _____

jive _____

kite _____

'th' beginning of words

the

than

that

thaw

thee

them

then

'th' beginning of words

they _____

thin _____

this _____

thud _____

thug _____

thus _____

thank _____

'y' end of words

any _____

icy _____

ivy _____

achy _____

army _____

baby _____

body _____

'y' end of words

bony _____

bury _____

busy _____

city _____

copy _____

dozy _____

duty _____

'tw' beginning of words

twig

twin

twang

tweak

tweed

tweet

twice

'tw' beginning of words

twine _____

twirl _____

twist _____

twelve _____

twenty _____

twinge _____

twitch _____

'ss' inside words

asset   _____

bossy   _____

essay   _____

fussy   _____

issue   _____

messy   _____

assent   _____

'ss' inside words

assert   _____

assess   _____

assign   _____

assist   _____

assume   _____

assure   _____

classy   _____

'll' inside words

ally

allay

alley

allow

alloy

bully

cello

'll' inside words

dolly   _____

folly   _____

fully   _____

gully   _____

hello   _____

hilly   _____

holly   _____

'oa'

oaf _____

oak _____

oat _____

boat _____

coat _____

coax _____

foal _____

'oa'

foam _____

goad _____

goat _____

hoax _____

load _____

loaf _____

loam _____

'oo' long

boo

coo

moo

too

zoo

boom

boot

'oo' long

cool   _____

coop   _____

doom   _____

food   _____

fool   _____

hoof   _____

hoop   _____

'oo' short

nook   _____

rook   _____

soot   _____

took   _____

wood   _____

woof   _____

wool   _____

'oo' short

brook _____

crook _____

shook _____

sooty _____

stood _____

cooker _____

cookie _____

"ea" as short e

dead

deaf

head

lead

ahead

bread

dealt

"ea" as short e

death   _____

dread   _____

heavy   _____

meant   _____

ready   _____

realm   _____

sweat   _____

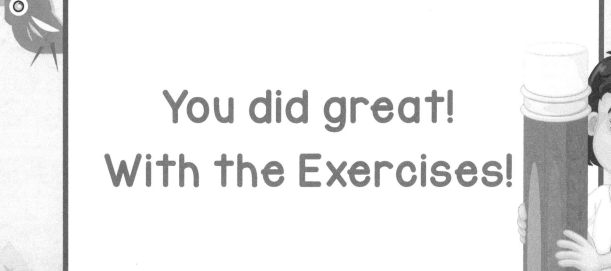
You did great!
With the Exercises!

9 781683 219507